Great Pyramid of Giza

by Grace Hansen

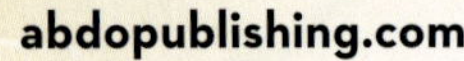

abdopublishing.com

Published by Abdo Kids, a division of ABDO, P.O. Box 398166, Minneapolis, Minnesota 55439.

Printed in the United States of America, North Mankato, Minnesota.

102017

012018

Photo Credits: Alamy, iStock, Shutterstock

Production Contributors: Teddy Borth, Jennie Forsberg, Grace Hansen

Design Contributors: Dorothy Toth, Laura Mitchell

Publisher's Cataloging in Publication Data

Names: Hansen, Grace, author.

Title: Great Pyramid of Giza / by Grace Hansen.

Description: Minneapolis, Minnesota : Abdo Kids, 2018. | Series: World wonders | Includes glossary, index and online resource (page 24).

Identifiers: LCCN 2017943151 | ISBN 9781532104404 (lib.bdg.) | ISBN 9781532105524 (ebook) | ISBN 9781532106088 (Read-to-me ebook)

Subjects: LCSH: Great Pyramid (Egypt)--Juvenile literature. | Pyramids of Giza (Egypt)--Juvenile literature. |Egypt--Antiquities--Juvenile literature. | Egypt--Civilization--to 332 BC--Juvenile literature.

Classification: DDC 932--dc23

LC record available at https://lccn.loc.gov/2017943151

Table of Contents

The Great Pyramid of Giza 4

The Giza Plateau 20

More Facts 22

Glossary 23

Index 24

Abdo Kids Code. 24

The Great Pyramid of Giza

The Great Pyramid of Giza is in Egypt. It is in the city Giza, which is near Cairo. Cairo is the capital of Egypt.

Egypt

Khufu was a **Pharaoh** in Egypt.

His rule began in 2589 BCE.

He wanted to be buried in an amazing tomb. He began building a massive pyramid.

The pyramid took nearly 20 years to complete. Around 20,000 people worked on it. It is said that Khufu treated his workers well.

The pyramid is made from around 2.3 million stones. Each stone weighs at least 2 tons (1,814 kg).

The pyramid's base is 754 feet (230 m) wide. It is 479 feet (146 m) tall! People today still do not know how it was built.

The pyramid once had a hidden door. Inside, there are still three main rooms. They are the king's chamber, the **Grand Gallery**, and the queen's chamber.

King's Chamber
Grand Gallery
Queen's Chamber
Entrance

The king's chamber is in the center of the pyramid. It once held Khufu's body. Khufu's treasures were in the pyramid too. But robbers took them long ago.

The Giza Plateau

There are three smaller pyramids near Khufu's. These are the tombs of his wives. The **Great Sphinx** is also nearby. Many people visit each year!

More Facts

- The Great Pyramid of Giza faces true north.

- The two larger pyramids near Khufu's belong to his son (Khafre) and grandson (Menkaure).

- No one is quite sure how the pyramid was built. But it is likely that ramps were built up to help place the massive stones.

Glossary

Grand Gallery – a 7 foot (2.1 m) wide and 153 foot (46.6 m) long passage that connects other smaller passages throughout the pyramid.

Great Sphinx – a massive limestone statue with the body of a lion and the head of a human. The face of the Sphinx is thought to be of Pharaoh Khafre, son of Khufu.

pharaoh – a king of ancient Egypt.

Index

building materials 12

build time 10

Cairo, Egypt 4

Egypt 4, 6

entrance 16

Giza, Egypt 4

Grand Gallery 16

Great Sphinx 20

Khufu 6, 8, 10, 18, 20

rooms 16, 18

size 12, 14

workers 10

Visit **abdokids.com** and use this code to access crafts, games, videos, and more!